SPIRITUAL WARFARE PRAYERS

ASH & PARCHMENT

ISBN: 979-8-9994652-0-7

Trademarks

For permissions, inquiries, or further information, please contact:

Ash & Parchment
8a Trolley Square
Wilmington, DE 19806
United States
Website: www.ashandparchment.com

✝

Spiritual Warfare Prayers

"For our struggle is not against flesh and blood, but against the rulers, against the authorities, against the powers of this dark world and against the spiritual forces of evil in the heavenly realms."

(Ephesians 6:12 NIV)

Table of Contents

Awakening to the Battle Within

Awakening to the Battle Within

You didn't stumble here by mistake. Something inside you has been stirring—quietly, persistently—whispering that life is meant to be more than just getting by. You've felt the pressure beneath the surface. The invisible weight pressing on your chest. The late-night thoughts that won't let you go. The ache of something missing, though you can't always name it.

This life feels heavy. And somewhere along the way, you began to wonder if God sees the weight you carry. If He hears the ache beneath your silence.

He does.

You're not weak for feeling like this. You're not broken for being tired. You're human. And you're in a battle—not against the world, but within your own heart.

But here's what no one told you: this war does not define you. And you are not alone in it. Jesus has already stepped into the very places where you now tremble. And He did not come to shame you. He came to stay.

This book won't fix you. But it will remind you of what's still true. Of the God who weeps with you, fights for you, and refuses to let go.

You don't have to rise all at once—just reach, and He'll meet you there.

The Invisible Battlefront

You may not realize it, but every day you wake up in the middle of a war. Not one with weapons or enemies you can see—but one fought in whispers, wounds, and thoughts that no one else hears.

It's a spiritual battle. A fight not against people or problems, but against the lies that tell you you're not loved, the fear that tries to paralyze you, and the shame that won't let you breathe.

Scripture reminds us:

"The weapons we fight with are not the weapons of the world. On the contrary, they have divine power to demolish strongholds." (2 Corinthians 10:4)

Heaven fights with you. His Word is your weapon. His presence is your shield. You don't need to see the battle to know that you've already been promised victory.

You were made to overcome.

And even in the unseen war, you are never fighting alone.

The Quiet Clash of Heart and Spirit

Spiritual warfare isn't always loud. Most days, it slips into your life quietly—in the hidden spaces of your mind and the quiet tension in your soul.

It looks like the steady pull of fear or anxiety that steals your peace before the day even begins. The temptation to believe you're not enough—not strong enough, not worthy enough, not truly loved.

It's the whisper of doubt that rises when life doesn't unfold the way you hoped. The lingering bitterness or quiet shame that holds you hostage to moments you wish you could forget.

But the enemy's power isn't endless. His reach is limited. And you are not left defenseless.

As a child of God, you've been given authority through Jesus to stand firm. You've been equipped to silence the lies, resist the pressure, and walk in truth—even when it's hard.

The clash may be quiet, but the outcome is sure.

And you are never fighting it alone.

Preparing for Spiritual Victory

Victory in the spiritual life doesn't begin with noise. It begins in stillness—when your heart quietly says yes to God before the battle even comes.

This isn't about trying harder. It's about trusting deeper. You don't have to prove your strength. You just have to position yourself where God can fight for you.

"Be still, and know that I am God." (Psalm 46:10)

The real preparation doesn't start when things go wrong—it starts in the secret place, where prayer becomes your breath and His Word becomes your anchor.

Before you fight the darkness around you, you must first silence the lies within you. That's why truth isn't optional—it's your foundation.

Here's how you prepare:

- Start with surrender. Strength comes after release.
- Stay in Scripture. It is your compass when emotions lie.
- Speak God's promises aloud. Faith grows when truth has a voice.
- Don't just pray for rescue—pray for resilience.

Your protection is spiritual, not situational. It doesn't depend on how calm life looks—it depends on where your heart is anchored.

God's covering isn't fragile. His armor wasn't made for perfect people—it was made for people who bleed, doubt, and still choose to stand.

"The name of the Lord is a strong tower; the righteous run to it and are safe." *(Proverbs 18:10)*

Speak Scripture out loud. When lies rise up, answer them with truth. God's Word is your sword—don't keep it sheathed.

Guard your thoughts. What you dwell on shapes what you believe. Stay close to what is good, pure, and trustworthy (Philippians 4:8).

Surround yourself with people who speak life. Spiritual battles are rarely won in isolation.

Worship, even when it hurts. Praise shifts the atmosphere within you before anything changes around you.

You may feel unqualified—but God has already equipped you.

Victory doesn't come from your power. It comes from His presence. And He's with you now.

How to Use This Prayer Guide Effectively

This prayer book is more than a collection of words; it's a companion for your spiritual journey, a sanctuary where your soul can find rest and renewal.

Begin with Intention
Approach each page with a heart ready to receive. Whether you're seeking solace, guidance, or simply a moment of peace, let your intention guide your reading.

Create a Sacred Space
Find a quiet corner where you can be alone with your thoughts and prayers. Light a candle, play soft instrumental music, or simply sit in silence. This space becomes your personal sanctuary.

Incorporate Scripture
Let the words of the Bible enrich your prayer experience. Reflect on passages that resonate with you, and allow them to deepen your understanding and connection.

Embrace the Rhythm
Establish a daily routine. Morning prayers can set the tone for your day, midday reflections can offer a moment of pause, and evening prayers can provide closure and gratitude.

Personalize Your Practice
Feel free to adapt the prayers to your personal experiences. Insert names, specific situations, or personal reflections to make each prayer uniquely yours.

Engage Your Senses
Read aloud to hear the words resonate. Write down prayers or thoughts in a journal. Use physical gestures like kneeling or raising your hands to embody your prayers.

Reflect and Listen
After each prayer, take a moment to sit in silence. Listen for any insights or feelings that arise. This practice, known as Lectio Divina, encourages a deeper communion with the divine.

Seek Community
Consider sharing this journey with others. Join a prayer group, discuss reflections with a friend, or participate in communal worship. Shared experiences can enrich your personal practice.

Remember, this prayer book is a tool to aid your spiritual journey. Use it in a way that feels authentic and nourishing to you. Let it be a source of comfort, inspiration, and connection.

Chapter 1:

Strength & Guidance

"But those who hope in the Lord will renew their strength.
They will soar on wings like eagles; they will run and not
grow weary, they will walk and not be faint."

(Isaiah 40:31 NIV)

Morning Prayer for Strength & Guidance

Heavenly Father,

Thank You for the gift of a new morning and for the chance to begin again in Your presence. I am grateful for life, for breath, and for the unseen ways You carried me through the night. As I rise, I open my heart to You, trusting that this day is not mine to control, but Yours to guide. You are my strength when I am weak and my light when the way ahead feels uncertain.

Lord, I place this day in Your hands. Lead me with wisdom and protect me from every plan of the enemy that would seek to distract or discourage me. Keep my mind focused on what is true, and my steps steady on the path You set before me. Let Your peace guard my heart, and let Your favor go before me in every decision, every conversation, and every place I set my foot. Fill me with discernment so I may recognize Your voice above all others, and give me courage to walk boldly in obedience.

When the weight of the day feels heavy, remind me that You are my refuge and my strength. Renew me with the power of Your Spirit so I do not grow weary or lose heart. Teach me to trust not in my own understanding but in Your unfailing wisdom. Let this day be marked by confidence, not in myself, but in who You are the God who goes before me, who walks beside me, and who holds every detail of my life.

~ In Jesus' name, Amen.

Prayer for Wisdom & Discernment

Heavenly Father,

I come before You with a heart that longs for Your wisdom. You are my Counselor, my Guide, and the One who sees the beginning and the end. Thank You for the gift of Your Spirit who teaches, corrects, and leads me in truth. I confess that without You, my understanding is limited, but with You, I can walk in clarity and peace.

Lord, I surrender my decisions, my thoughts, and my plans into Your hands. Protect me from confusion and deception, and silence every voice that would lead me away from Your will. Guard my heart against distractions and wrong paths, and give me discernment to recognize what is good and what is harmful. Let Your wisdom shape my words, my choices, and my relationships, so that all I do reflects Your truth.

When the way forward feels uncertain, steady me with Your presence. Open my eyes to see where You are leading, and give me courage to follow even when I don't fully understand. Let my heart be anchored in trust, knowing that You order my steps and guide me into what is best. I choose to rely not on myself but on You alone, believing that You will make my path straight.

~ In Jesus' name, Amen.

Prayer for Strength in Times of Trials

Heavenly Father,

In moments of trial and uncertainty, I lift my heart to You. You are my Rock, my Refuge, and my Strength. Thank You for being present in every storm, holding me when I feel weak and reminding me that I am never alone. Though the weight of life presses in, I choose to lean on You, trusting that Your hand upholds me and Your presence sustains me.

Lord, I surrender the heaviness I carry. Replace discouragement with courage, fear with faith, and weakness with endurance. Protect my mind from lies that tell me I cannot make it, and silence every attack that seeks to shake my peace. Teach me to see these challenges not as defeat but as opportunities for growth, shaping me into who You have called me to be. Let patience rise within me, and let perseverance finish its work so that I may stand strong, complete, and rooted in You.

Even when the storm rages, I will not be moved. You are my ever-present help, my steady anchor when everything else feels uncertain. Strengthen me to endure with hope, and remind me that victory is already mine in Christ. This trial will not define me, it will refine me. With You, I can stand firm, unshaken, and filled with courage to overcome.

~ In Jesus' name, Amen.

Chapter 2:

Peace & Protection

"So do not fear, for I am with you; do not be dismayed, for I am your God. I will strengthen you and help you; I will uphold you with my righteous right hand."

(Isaiah 41:10 NIV)

Prayer of the Soul: Anima Christi

Heavenly Father,

I come before You, grateful for the life, death, and resurrection of Jesus Christ. Through Him I find cleansing, healing, and strength. Thank You for the gift of His body that saves me, His blood that redeems me, and His love that draws me close. I cannot earn this grace, but I receive it with humility and thanksgiving, knowing that in Christ I am made whole.

Lord Jesus, cover me with Your presence. Hide me in Your wounds, where I am safe from every attack of the enemy. Wash me in Your mercy and strengthen me in my weakness. When I feel fragile, remind me that Your suffering has already secured my victory. When fear rises, let Your Spirit shield me and keep me from being separated from You.

At the close of my life, call me to Yourself. Let me finish this journey held in Your arms, and welcome me into the eternal joy of Your presence. Until that day, help me to walk faithfully, to love deeply, and to honor You with my life. May my soul find its rest in You alone, and may my voice join with the saints in praise forevermore.

~ In Jesus' name, Amen.

Praying Psalm 91

Heavenly Father,

I come to You with open hands and a heart ready to trust. The world may shake, but You remain unshaken. You are my hiding place, my shelter from every storm. I don't come in fear. I come in faith, believing that when I draw near to You, I am covered, safe, and held.

I may not know what tomorrow brings, but I know who holds me. I may not see the path ahead, but I know Your wings are spread over me. You promise to deliver, to shield, to rescue and I believe You.

You are not distant or silent.
You are near, and You are mighty.

Wrap me in the warmth of Your protection. Let Your truth be my armor and Your presence my peace. Send Your angels to lift me up when I stumble, to guard the way before me, and to remind me that I am never alone.

In You, fear turns to courage. Shadows break into light.
You are my refuge, my fortress, my God in whom I trust.

~ In Jesus' name, Amen.

Prayer for Protection Against Spiritual Attacks

Heavenly Father,

I come before You in the name of Jesus, knowing that even when darkness tries to surround me, You are my light. You see what I cannot see. You fight battles I do not understand. And I trust that no force of evil can stand against You.

Lord, I recognize the weight that presses in.

Sometimes it feels like fear comes out of nowhere. My thoughts grow heavy, my peace is shaken, and I feel like I'm under attack. But I will not let fear rule over me. I will not agree with the lies of the enemy. You are my refuge.

I will not bow to fear. I will not surrender to what is not from You. You are my Defender and Deliverer. You are greater than anything that comes against me. Your presence is my stronghold, and I will stand firm.

I surrender every fear to You, Lord. Strengthen me, protect me, and fill me with Your peace.

I trust You more than I trust my fear.

~ In Jesus' name, Amen.

Prayer for Peace & Protection Throughout the Day

Heavenly Father

As I begin this day, I place every worry, every fear, and every burden into Your hands. Thank You for being my refuge and my fortress, the One I can trust no matter what comes. You are my shield and my protector, and I rest in the assurance that Your presence surrounds me. Wherever I go, You go before me, and Your love keeps me steady.

Lord, cover me with Your protection and keep me safe from harm. Guard my heart from distractions that would steal my peace, and silence every scheme of the enemy that seeks to bring confusion or fear. Let Your angels watch over me and those I love, guiding our steps and protecting our paths. Fill my mind with clarity, and let my heart remain steadfast in trust, knowing that nothing can separate me from Your care.

Father, I ask for Your peace to rest upon me throughout this day. Let no situation shake my confidence in You. Keep my thoughts anchored in Your goodness, and my spirit secure in Your presence. May I walk in calmness and courage, covered by Your favor and strengthened by Your grace. Thank You for being my safe place, my constant help, and my everlasting peace.

~ In Jesus' name, Amen.

Prayer for Overcoming Anxiety & Stress

Heavenly Father,

I come to You with the weight of my worries and the thoughts that will not rest. At times, fear feels louder than faith, and my heart struggles to find stillness. Yet even in the middle of my restlessness, I turn to You. Thank You for being my refuge and my peace, the One who never grows weary of carrying what I cannot bear.

Lord, I lay every anxious thought at Your feet. Quiet the noise that floods my mind and calm the storm that rises in my spirit. Break the grip of fear that tries to hold me, and silence the lies that tell me I am not enough. Protect me from the heaviness that seeks to steal my joy, and surround me with the assurance of Your presence.

Teach me to breathe in Your peace when anxiety presses close. Remind me that I do not face this battle alone. That You are my strength when I am weak, my calm when I feel shaken, and my hope when the future feels uncertain. Replace my fear with courage, my stress with rest, and my worry with trust.

Thank You, Lord, for being near to me in every moment of struggle. Anchor my heart in Your love and steady my mind in Your truth. I choose to walk in Your peace, confident that no matter what comes, You are with me and You will not let me go.

~ In Jesus' name, Amen.

Prayer to Release Control & Trust God

Heavenly Father,

I often find myself gripping tightly to what I think I can control. I plan, I push, I try to hold everything together, but deep down, I know that much of life is beyond me. And that truth humbles me. I don't want to carry what was never mine to bear. I want to trust You with what I can't see.

There are parts of my story that feel unfinished. Moments I wish made more sense. Doors that haven't opened. Paths that look unclear. It's hard to move forward when the next step feels hidden. But I believe You are leading me, even when I don't understand the way.

Lord, help me release my need to control.

Quiet the thoughts that keep circling in my mind. Remind me that surrender is not weakness, it's worship. Fill the space left by fear with faith in Your goodness. Teach me to rest in the truth that You are already working, even when I can't see the outcome.

I walk forward, not because I see the way, but because I know You are with me.

~ In Jesus' name, Amen.

Prayer for Surrendering to God's Will

Heavenly Father,

So much of life feels beyond my reach. Unanswered questions, uncertain days, and moments where everything feels fragile. I try to hold it all together, but my strength is not enough. I need You to steady me.

Lord, I open my hands and release what was never mine to control. I lay down my striving, my anxious thoughts, and the weight of trying to figure everything out. Wrap me in Your peace, the kind that quiets storms and stills restless hearts. Remind me that surrender isn't failure, it's faith.

Lead me one step at a time. Even when the path is hidden, let me trust Your voice more than my fear. Plant courage where uncertainty lives, and help me find joy not just in answers, but in walking beside You.

You are my anchor in the unknown. My future rests safely in Your hands. When I'm tempted to take back control, remind me that You've never let me go.

Thank You for being the God who carries what I can't.
In You, I find peace and I surrender again.

~ In Jesus' name, Amen.

Chapter 3:

Inner Pain & Healing

"Come to me, all you who are weary and burdened, and I will give you rest. Take my yoke upon you and learn from me, for I am gentle and humble in heart, and you will find rest for your souls. For my yoke is easy and my burden is light."

(Matthew 11:28–30 NIV)

Prayer for God's Presence in Isolation

Heavenly Father,

There are moments when the silence feels louder than any noise. When the room is still, and I'm left alone with my thoughts, it's easy to wonder if anyone sees or understands. But in this quiet, I turn my heart toward You. You are the One who never leaves. The One who is near, even when no one else is.

Loneliness has a way of whispering lies. It says I've been forgotten. It tells me I'm invisible. But You, Lord, remind me of what is true. That I am seen, known, and deeply loved by You. You are not far off; You are here.

You are the God who sits with me in silence.
The One who understands what my heart cannot say.

Wrap me in Your presence, Lord. Let me feel Your nearness in a tangible way. Fill the quiet with Your peace. Speak gently to my soul and remind me that I belong to You. Help me to recognize that Your companionship is not second-best, it is the greatest gift I could receive.

Thank You for being the One who sees me, stays with me, and loves me fully. With You, I am never truly alone.

~ In Jesus' name, Amen.

Prayer for Connection & Belonging

Heavenly Father,

You created us to live in relationship, with You and with others. But right now, my heart feels distant and disconnected. I find myself longing to be seen, understood, and welcomed. I crave real connection, yet I often feel like I'm on the outside looking in.

There are moments when I wonder if I truly fit anywhere.

I carry the ache of feeling invisible or misunderstood, even in a room full of people. But even in that pain, I turn to You. You see me fully.

Lord, guide me toward the relationships You have prepared for me.

Open the doors to friendships that are honest, life-giving, and rooted in Your truth. Help me to step forward with courage when connection feels risky. Teach me not to fear vulnerability, but to trust that You are working even in the waiting.

Remind me that I am chosen by You, not by accident, but with purpose. Let Your love anchor me when the world feels distant. With You, I am always known. With You, I always belong.

~ In Jesus' name, Amen.

Prayer for Comfort in Grief

Heavenly Father,

I come to You in a place I never wanted to be. Empty, aching, and overwhelmed by the loss of someone I love so deeply. Nothing feels the same. The world keeps turning, but mine has stopped.

God, I need You now more than ever.

I lay my grief at Your feet, not because it's small or easy, but because I cannot carry it alone. Wrap Your arms around me and hold me when I feel like falling apart.

Lord, I miss them so much. The sound of their voice, the way they smiled, the way they made life feel lighter. I don't know how to live without that light. I ask for your presence here. Sit with me and help me remember that death is not the end.

Because of You, love endures. Because of You, this goodbye is not forever. Because of You, one day, all things will be made new including this shattered heart of mine.

Until that day, hold me. Don't let go of me.

~ In Jesus' name, Amen.

Prayer for Emotional Restoration

Heavenly Father,

There are places in my heart that still ache. Wounds I carry in silence, too deep for words. Pain from the past, quiet disappointments, and unspoken struggles have left me tired, worn, and unsure of how to move forward. But I know You see it all. You understand what I can't explain, and You hold what I can't carry.

Lord, step into the ruins of my heart and breathe life again.

Bring Your healing into the corners of my soul that feel forgotten. Where sorrow has settled, plant seeds of joy. Where bitterness has grown, pour out grace. Where fear lingers, let Your peace take root.

Teach me to release what I've buried. Help me to let go of anger, to forgive where I've been wounded, and to open my heart again, this time, to You. Let Your love fill every empty space, and remind me that I am never alone in my pain.

Thank You for being near to the brokenhearted. You are my comfort, my safe place, and the one who makes all things new. I trust that You are healing me, even now, one moment at a time.

~ In Jesus' name, Amen.

Strength to Endure Sickness

Heavenly Father,

You are my Healer, the One who brought restoration to the weary, sight to the blind, and strength to the broken. Today, I come to You with my pain, my weakness, and every part of me that needs Your touch.

Strengthen me from within. Let Your presence renew every part of my body that feels tired and worn. Breathe life into my cells, energy into my limbs, and peace into my heart. Drive out all that does not belong, and fill me with wholeness and rest.

Lord, when healing feels distant, hold me close. Quiet the restless thoughts that cloud my hope, and calm my anxious thoughts and let Your peace settle deep within me. Wrap me in the deep assurance that You are working, even in what I cannot yet see.

Bless those who care for me, Lord. Guide the hands that offer treatment and comfort. Let their words bring reassurance and their presence reflect Your compassion. May every act of care be touched by Your grace.

I give You all my fears, Lord, and rest in the quiet hope that You are healing me, even now.

~ In Jesus' name, Amen.

Chapter 4:

Addiction, Cycles & Freedom

"No temptation has overtaken you except what is common to mankind. And God is faithful; he will not let you be tempted beyond what you can bear. But when you are tempted, he will also provide a way out so that you can endure it."

(1 Corinthians 10:13 NIV)

Prayer to Break Addictive Patterns

Heavenly Father,

You see the battle I face, the cycle I keep falling into, even when my heart longs for freedom. These habits have held me captive, and I confess that I feel tired of trying to fight on my own. But I know You are stronger than anything that tries to control me.

You know the pain behind it, the shame that follows it, and the hunger beneath it. And still, You love me. You call me worthy of healing and capable of change through Your power. You don't condemn me. You invite me to rise.

In the name of Jesus, I speak freedom over my life.

Break the chains I've tried to carry alone. Fill the empty places with Your Spirit, so that what once tempted me now loses its grip. Give me the strength to say no, and the courage to walk toward wholeness, one step at a time.

Let Your Word renew my mind. Let Your grace cover every failure. And when I feel weak, remind me that Your strength is made perfect right there, in the place of my need. Thank You for never giving up on me.

~ In Jesus' name, Amen.

Prayer for Strength Against Temptation

Heavenly Father,

You know the moments when temptation feels close, when I am tired, uncertain, or alone. It comes quietly sometimes, dressed as comfort or escape. But deep down, I know it leads me away from You. I don't want to keep giving in. I want to stand firm in Your strength.

You see every thought, every decision, every tug-of-war inside me. And You have not left me to fight alone. Your Spirit is within me, and Your power is greater than whatever tries to pull me away.

Lord, open my eyes when temptation comes.

Help me to see clearly what it is and where it leads. Show me the way out You have promised, and give me the courage to take it. Let my desire for You grow stronger than anything that tries to replace You.

Fill my heart with Your presence, so there's no room left for what doesn't belong. And when I fall, remind me I can get back up, because Your grace never ends. Thank You for being my strength, my shield, and my victory. With You, I can overcome.

~ In Jesus' name, Amen.

Prayer for Renewal & Freedom

Heavenly Father,

You know the weight I've been carrying. The mistakes I regret, the habits I want to leave behind, the thoughts that keep telling me I'll never change. But I come to You today, not to stay stuck, but to begin again. Because with You, freedom is possible, and new beginnings are real.

Restore my heart, Lord, and refresh my mind.

Lift the heaviness of guilt and fill those empty spaces with the light of Your mercy. Let me feel the beauty of being made new. Not because of what I've done, but because of who You are.

Plant hope where fear has lived too long. Let Your peace take root deep within me. Teach me to walk in grace, one decision at a time, trusting that even the smallest steps matter when I walk with You.

Thank You for being patient with me in this journey. When I grow weary, be my strength. When I forget who I am, remind me I am Yours. You are not just giving me a second chance, you are giving me a new beginning.

Because of You, I can rise again. Because of You, I am free.

~ In Jesus' name, Amen.

Chapter 5:

Relationships & Family

"Above all, clothe yourselves with love, which binds us all together in perfect harmony."

(Colossians 3:14 NIV)

Restore What's Been Broken

Heavenly Father,

You see the wounds within my relationships. The quiet ache left by harsh words, missed understanding, and wounds that time has not yet healed. Relationships that once brought comfort now carry the weight of silence and pain. But I believe You are the God who restores, who takes what's fractured and makes it whole again.

Lord, teach me how to forgive when my heart resists.

Soften the edges of my pride and sweep out the bitterness that tries to linger. Help me release the need to be right, and instead, choose the higher path of love and peace. Let Your compassion fill me so I can see others through Your eyes.

Guide me in the gentle work of healing. Give me wisdom to speak with care, courage to take the first step, and patience for the slow rebuilding of trust.

You showed us that no rift is too wide, no heart too stubborn for Your redemption. Restore not only what's between us, Lord, but what's broken within me too.

~ In Jesus' name, Amen.

Prayer for Finding Balance in Relationships

Heavenly Father,

You have called me to walk in love. Real, selfless, grace-filled love. Yet at times, in the giving, I feel myself slowly fading. I long to care well, to offer kindness freely, but I sometimes forget that You've also asked me to guard the heart You made.

Lord, teach me how to love with both open hands and steady boundaries.

Show me how to offer compassion without losing clarity. Let my "yes" come from peace, and my "no" be rooted in wisdom. Shape my limits not out of fear or self-preservation, but from the sacred place of knowing who I am in You.

Open my eyes to see what draws me closer to You, and what slowly pulls me away. Give me courage to walk away with grace when needed, and strength to nurture what is good, holy, and whole. Let love flow both ways, marked by respect, truth, and gentleness.

Shape me into someone who loves deeply and wisely. Secure in Your truth, rooted in Your peace, and always led by Your Spirit. And Lord, may I never love anything more than I love You.

~ In Jesus' name, Amen.

Prayer for Strength to Move On

Heavenly Father,

Letting go is one of the hardest paths You call us to. When love changes or fades, it leaves behind an ache that words can't quite carry. Yet in the shadows of goodbye, I trust that You still hold the whole story, and that no ending is wasted in Your hands.

Lord, help me release what I cannot hold together.

Give me strength to let go without resentment, and to trust that surrender is not defeat, but a doorway into Your greater purpose. Quiet the fears that beg me to cling, and open my heart to the peace that follows obedience.

Where loss has hollowed out spaces in me, fill them with Your presence. Let Your love be the anchor when I feel adrift. Be my steady place when emotions shift, and my light when the road ahead is unclear.

Thank You for walking beside me through every ending and new beginning. Lead me forward, not with haste, but with hope. Let this parting make room for new beginnings. Crafted by Your hand, rooted in peace, and marked by joy.

~ In Jesus' name, Amen.

Prayer for Family Restoration

Heavenly Father,

You see what lies behind every closed door. The distance created by misunderstandings, the wounds left by careless words, and the silence that has replaced connection. Yet You are the Healer of hearts, the Mender of what we cannot fix on our own.

Let Your peace settle gently over this home, Lord. Where anger once rose, let patience grow. Where resentment lingered, sow forgiveness. Let Your love take root in every room, pushing out every trace of fear, division, and bitterness.

Teach us to see each other through eyes of grace. Soften what has grown hard. Restore what time has frayed. Give us words that build rather than break, and hearts willing to listen, to forgive, and to begin again.

Break every cycle of pain and replace it with patterns of compassion and truth. May this family be shaped not by the past, but by Your promises. Knit us together with cords of faith and mercy that cannot be torn.

Thank You, Lord, that no wound is too deep and no home too far gone for You to restore.

~ In Jesus' name, Amen.

Nighttime Prayer for Rest & Renewal

Heavenly Father,

As this day comes to a close, I lift my heart to You in gratitude. Thank You for carrying me through every moment. For Your guidance when I felt uncertain, for Your protection when I felt vulnerable, and for Your provision in ways I may not have even noticed. Tonight, I lay down my cares and release every burden into Your hands, trusting that You are faithful to watch over me as I sleep.

Lord, calm my mind and quiet my heart. Remove the weight of anxious thoughts and silence the fears that try to rise in the night. Cover me with Your presence and let Your peace rest over this room like a blanket of safety. Protect me from anything that would disturb my rest, and guard my dreams so that my spirit remains at peace.

I surrender every worry to You, knowing that You are in control even while I sleep. Fill me with deep, restorative rest that renews my body and refreshes my soul. Let my sleep be free of fear, free of restlessness, and filled only with the assurance of Your love. When morning comes, awaken me with clarity, strength, and joy, ready to step into a new day with confidence in You.

Thank You for being the Keeper of my nights and the Giver of my peace. I rest securely in Your care, trusting that I am never alone and never outside of Your protection.

~ In Jesus' name, Amen.

Chapter 6:

Curses & Family Struggles

"Christ redeemed us from the curse of the law by becoming a curse for us, for it is written: 'Cursed is everyone who is hung on a pole.'"

(Galatians 3:13 NIV)

Breaking Generational Curses

Heavenly Father,

In the name of Jesus, the Name above every name, I come to You with faith that breaks chains. You are my Redeemer and Defender, and by the power of the cross and the blood that flowed from it, I stand in the authority You've given me.

I speak to every curse spoken and every shadow passed down, be broken in Jesus' name.

No dark word, no hidden vow, no ancient bondage has claim over me. Whatever has traveled through generations to burden or bind, I now lay at the foot of the cross. Let every whispered lie and unholy thread unravel in Your presence.

I renounce every agreement made in fear, every path once walked in darkness, known or unknown. Forgive the sins of my fathers, Lord, and wash my bloodline clean. Let the wounds of the past be healed by Your mercy, and every door once opened to the enemy be shut by Your hand.

I walk forward now, not as one bound by the past, but as a child of freedom, written into a new legacy of grace and glory.

~ In Jesus' name, Amen.

Prayer for Breaking Soul Ties and Unholy Connections

Heavenly Father,

I come before You in the mighty name of Jesus Christ, my Redeemer and Deliverer. Thank You for being the One who sets captives free and breaks every chain. Today I bring before You every soul tie, every toxic connection, and every spiritual attachment that is not from You. I refuse to remain bound by anything that pulls me away from Your presence.

In the authority of Jesus' name, I declare that every chain of bondage, every unhealthy attachment, and every lingering tie from my past is broken. I sever every connection that drains my spirit, delays my purpose, or clouds my mind. What once held me no longer has power over me. I take back my peace, my purity, my joy, and my destiny, restored and covered by the blood of Jesus.

Lord, heal the places where these ties have wounded me. Restore my heart from every scar and fill the empty spaces with Your Spirit.

From this moment forward, I stand in freedom. I am no longer bound. I am whole, I am healed, and I am covered in Your power. Every chain is broken, every tie is cut, and I walk forward in the authority of Christ, secure in Your truth and unshakable in Your love.

~ In Jesus' name, Amen.

Prayer to to Cancel Evil Words Spoken Against Me

Heavenly Father,

I come before You in the mighty name of Jesus Christ, the Word made flesh and the Lord above every name. Thank You that Your plans for me stand firm and that no lie or spoken word can ultimately overturn Your purpose. Today I take my place in the authority of Christ and declare that every evil decree, every word curse, and every negative declaration spoken over my life is canceled, reversed, and destroyed right now. I will not carry the labels of the enemy. I refuse every lie that has tried to shape my destiny.

By the power of Jesus' blood and the authority given to me in His name, I break and overturn every spoken curse, every false prophecy, and every demonic word formed against my health, my family, my finances, and my calling. I revoke every assignment of hatred, envy, and witchcraft. I call back every fragment of myself that was stolen by words and transfer it back into wholeness. Let every tongue raised against me be silenced. Let every scheme spoken in secret be exposed, nullified, and returned to its sender.

Father, establish Your voice over mine and set Your blessing upon my life. From this moment forward I walk in divine favor, breakthrough, and supernatural vindication. No curse will find purchase, no decree will stand, and no lie will shape my future. My name is written in the book of life and my path is secured by Your hand. I step forward in faith, believing that what You have spoken over me will prosper and stand.

~ In Jesus' name, Amen.

Prayer to Block Evil Eyes & Listening Spirits

Heavenly Father,

I come before You in the mighty name of Jesus Christ, my Defender and Shield. You see what is hidden in the dark and expose the plans of the enemy. Tonight I bring before You every spirit assigned to monitor, record, or invade my life. I refuse to live under fear or surveillance. Shine Your light into every hidden place and let every scheme against me be revealed and destroyed.

By the authority of Jesus' name, I break and dismantle every assignment of monitoring, every demonic watcher, and every network sent to track my steps. I cancel all illegal access to my mind, my home, and my family. I command every spirit of surveillance and intrusion to be unmasked, bound, and cast out. Let every plan be nullified, every weapon disarmed, and every attempt to control me be turned back on its sender. By the blood of Jesus, I take back every part of my life that has been stolen.

Cover me, Lord, with Your presence and place a hedge of protection around me and those I love. Surround us with Your angels and hide us in the shelter of Your wings. Give me discernment to recognize deception and boldness to walk in the authority You have given me. From this moment forward, I stand secure and unshakable. No hidden watcher will prevail, and no secret scheme will prosper. I walk in freedom, protection, and victory.

~ In Jesus' name, Amen.

Prayer to Destroy Dark Powers Raised Against Me

Heavenly Father,

I come before You in the mighty name of Jesus Christ, the Consuming Fire and Lord of Hosts. Thank You for being the One who defends me, covers me, and fights for me. Today I rise in the authority of Christ and declare that every altar of darkness raised against my life, my family, or my destiny is consumed by Your fire. No altar built in secret, no sacrifice spoken in my name, and no ritual formed against me will stand in Your presence.

By the blood of Jesus, I tear down every altar of witchcraft, delay, sickness, financial struggle, fear, or oppression that has been raised to limit me. I nullify every sacrifice made against me and declare it powerless. Let every altar that speaks my name, my purpose, or my household be silenced now. I command every evil assignment to be canceled, reversed, and sent back to its source. What the enemy intended for harm will not take root, for You have already secured my victory.

Father, release Your fire to consume every shrine, every ritual, and every plan of darkness that has opposed me. Surround me and those I love with divine protection and cover us under the blood of Jesus. From this moment forward, I walk in freedom, strength, and breakthrough. No altar of darkness will ever prevail against me. My life, my destiny, and my future are secured in Christ alone.

~ In Jesus' name, Amen.

Prayer to Break Yokes
of Bondage and Oppression

Heavenly Father,

I come before You in the mighty name of Jesus Christ, my Deliverer and Chain Breaker. Thank You for being my refuge and strong tower, the One who lifts every burden and destroys every yoke of oppression. Today I rise in the authority of Christ and declare that every chain holding me back is broken. Every stronghold, every burden, and every form of spiritual captivity that has tried to weigh me down is shattered by the power of Your name.

In the authority of Jesus, I command every spiritual prison to open and every demonic chain to fall. I destroy the yokes of fear, depression, addiction, financial struggle, sickness, and generational curses. Every assignment of bondage is broken now, and every stronghold of darkness is torn down. What the enemy has used to oppress me will no longer hold me captive. I declare that my mind, my body, my spirit, and my destiny are free, redeemed, and covered in the blood of Jesus.

Lord, fill the places where oppression once lived with Your Spirit. Cover me with peace, joy, and strength. Let Your anointing destroy every yoke and release me into liberty and victory. From this moment forward, I walk in freedom. No more captivity, no more chains, no more oppression. I step boldly into the life You have prepared for me, covered in Your power and unshakable in Your truth.

~ In Jesus' name, Amen.

Prayer Against Witchcraft
& Occult Attacks

Heavenly Father,

I come before You in the mighty name of Jesus Christ, my Lord and Savior, declaring that my life belongs to You alone. Thank You that no spell, curse, or occult work can prevail against the power of Your blood. Today I rise in my God-given authority and stand against every work of witchcraft, sorcery, and occult activity sent to harm, hinder, or confuse me. I decree that my life, my family, and my destiny are secured in Your hands, not in the hands of the enemy.

By the authority of Jesus Christ, I cancel and nullify every ritual, incantation, and evil decree spoken over me. I destroy every altar, every enchantment, and every assignment meant to bind or control me. I rebuke every monitoring spirit, every spirit of manipulation, and every power of darkness working against my peace and progress. I declare that every chain, snare, and trap is broken now, and every plan of the enemy is overturned. No weapon formed against me shall prosper, for I am covered and protected by the blood of Jesus.

Father, let Your fire consume every spirit of witchcraft, every demonic contract, and every evil force that rises against me. Surround me with Your angels and place a hedge of divine protection around my life, my home, and my family. From this day forward, I walk in total victory, unshakable protection, and supernatural favor. I declare in the name of Jesus Christ that I am untouchable, unmovable, and unstoppable.

~ In Jesus' name, Amen.

Chapter 7:

Silent Struggles

"Come to me, all you who are weary and burdened, and I will give you rest. Take my yoke upon you and learn from me, for I am gentle and humble in heart, and you will find rest for your souls."

(Matthew 11:28–29 NIV)

Prayer for Breaking
the Spirit of Rejection

Heavenly Father,

You are the God who calls me chosen, beloved, and accepted in Christ. Thank You that before the foundation of the world, You knew me, formed me, and set Your love upon me. Though others may have turned away, misjudged me, or cast me aside, You have never abandoned me. Your Word declares that nothing can separate me from the love of Christ, and I hold fast to that truth.

Lord, I come against every lie of the enemy that whispers I am unwanted, unworthy, or unloved. I reject the weight of rejection that has tried to settle in my heart, and I renounce the power of shame, insecurity, and fear that come with it. By the blood of Jesus Christ, I declare that rejection has no authority over me. I belong to You, and Your acceptance is greater than man's rejection.

Father, heal the wounds of my past where rejection cut deep. Restore my identity in Your truth and anchor my heart in Your unchanging love. Teach me to walk with confidence, knowing I am a child of God, chosen and appointed for good works. Let Your Spirit fill the empty spaces where rejection once lived, and replace them with peace, belonging, and joy.

I declare today that I am not forsaken. I am not forgotten. I am fully loved, fully accepted, and fully secure in Christ Jesus.

In Jesus' name, Amen.

Prayer for Breaking Shame & Condemnation

Heavenly Father,

Thank You for the gift of salvation through Jesus Christ. Thank You that His blood has cleansed me, His cross has set me free, and His resurrection has secured my victory. Even when guilt and shame rise up against me, Your Word declares that there is no condemnation for those who are in Christ Jesus. I praise You that my worth is not measured by my past mistakes, but by the finished work of the cross.

Lord, I renounce every voice of shame and every chain of condemnation that has tried to bind my heart. I break agreement with the lies of the enemy that tell me I am unworthy, dirty, or beyond redemption. By the authority of Jesus Christ, I silence every accusation and cancel every record of wrongs nailed to the cross. The power of shame is broken, and I step into the covering of Your grace.

Father, wash me again in Your mercy. Heal the wounds left by regret and release me from the weight of self-condemnation. Teach me to see myself through Your eyes—redeemed, restored, and made new. Let the light of Your truth shine in every hidden place, driving out the darkness of shame and filling me with the confidence of Your love.

I declare that I am forgiven, I am free, and I am made whole in Jesus. Shame has no hold on me, and condemnation cannot accuse me. I walk forward clothed in righteousness, secure in the mercy of my Savior.

~ In Jesus' name, Amen.

Prayer for When I Feel Like Giving Up

Heavenly Father,

Thank You that You see me in my weakness and that Your heart is tender toward the tired. Thank You for the times You have carried me when I could not carry myself, for the rest You have offered in the midst of my struggle, and for the patience You show when I stumble. Even now, I am grateful that You are near and that Your love does not depend on my strength.

Lord, I confess that I feel tired and tempted to surrender. Forgive me for the times I've doubted Your goodness or allowed despair to silence my hope. I lay down shame, fear, and discouragement, and I ask for Your mercy to cover me.

Father, I need You now more than ever. Reach into the place where I feel like giving up and breathe hope there. Lift the weight from my shoulders, steady my feet, and remind me of the small next step You would have me take. Replace my despair with renewed purpose; teach me to rest in Your promises when the road feels too long. Give me courage to ask for help, wisdom to receive it, and the humility to keep coming back to You even when I fail.

I surrender this wanting-to-give-up to You. Restore my weary soul, remind me who I am in Christ, and rekindle the quiet faith that will keep me moving even when I cannot see the finish line.

~ In Jesus' name, Amen.

Prayer for Battles No One Sees

Heavenly Father,

You see the tears I don't let fall, the weight I don't speak of, and the battles I fight in silence. Thank You that nothing is hidden from You. Not the heaviness I carry in the quiet, not the ache behind my smile, not the nights when I feel like I'm breaking inside. You know me fully, and still You call me loved.

Lord, I confess that I've tried to be strong on my own, but inside I feel weary and afraid. The enemy whispers that no one would understand, that I'm too weak, too broken, too far gone. But I refuse to agree with those lies. In the name of Jesus, I break the power of shame, fear, and secrecy over my life. I declare that I do not fight alone, for You are with me, even in the shadows.

Father, wrap me in Your presence when I feel unseen. Hold me when I cannot hold myself. Speak Your truth into the places where lies have settled, and breathe hope into the corners of my heart where despair has tried to live. Teach me to rest in the promise that I am fully known and never abandoned.

I declare today that my hidden battles will not destroy me. Instead, they will become places where Your strength is revealed. What was meant to silence me will become a testimony of Your faithfulness. Even here, in the struggles no one else sees, I am loved, I am held, and I am victorious in Christ.

~ In Jesus' name, Amen.

Prayer for Secret Wounds

Heavenly Father,

You see the places in me that no one else does. The scars I've hidden, the pain I've buried, and the wounds I've carried in silence. Thank You that nothing is too hidden for Your healing, and no part of me is too broken for Your love. Even in the places I try to cover, You draw near with compassion and mercy.

Lord, I confess that I've carried secret hurts for too long. Words that cut deep, losses I never spoke of, regrets that linger in the dark. Shame told me to keep them hidden, but silence has only made the pain grow heavier. Today, I bring them into Your light. In the name of Jesus, I break every lie that says I must carry these wounds alone. I declare that what was hidden in darkness will be healed in Your presence.

Father, pour out Your Spirit on the deepest places of my heart. Touch the wounds that still ache, the memories that still sting, and the brokenness that feels beyond repair. Replace every shadow of shame with the light of Your truth. Let Your love soak into every scar until what once felt like weakness becomes a testimony of Your grace.

I declare that my secret wounds will not define me. I am not marked by pain, but by redemption. I am not bound by shame, but covered in mercy. What was once hidden will now reveal the depth of Your healing power. My story will not end in brokenness, but in restoration.

~ In Jesus' name, Amen.

Chapter 8:

Finances & Career

"But seek first his kingdom and his righteousness, and all these
things will be given to you as well."

(Matthew 6:33 NIV)

Prayer for Work, Business & Career Success

Heavenly Father,

I come before You in the mighty name of Jesus Christ, the God of abundance and favor. Thank You for being the One who blesses the work of my hands and establishes my steps. Today I surrender my career, my business, and every professional endeavor into Your hands, trusting that You alone bring success and prosperity. I declare that my hands are blessed, my labor will not be in vain, and everything I set my heart to do will prosper.

By the authority of Jesus Christ, I cancel every spirit of lack, stagnation, and delay that has tried to block my advancement. I break every demonic barrier standing in the way of my promotion, my increase, and my opportunities. I declare that open doors of favor are being released, and every closed path that is not from You is removed. My work will not be hindered, my business will not be limited, and my career will not be held back. I will rise and excel, bringing glory to Your name.

Father, guide me to walk in diligence, wisdom, and integrity so that my work may reflect Your goodness. Let my efforts be fruitful, my business expand, and my career advance in ways that testify of Your hand upon my life. From this moment forward, I operate in divine success. I step into supernatural breakthroughs, new opportunities, and lasting prosperity, knowing that my future is secured in You.

~ In Jesus' name, Amen.

Prayer for Divine Favor & Opportunities

Heavenly Father,

I come before You in the mighty name of Jesus Christ, the God of open doors and breakthroughs. Thank You for being the One who goes before me and makes a way where there seems to be none. Today I ask for Your favor to surround me like a shield. Let Your grace rest upon my life, opening doors that no man can shut and positioning me in places of blessing, increase, and divine opportunity.

By the authority of Jesus Christ, I cancel every spirit of delay, rejection, and denial that has tried to block my advancement. I command every closed door assigned against my destiny to open now. I break every chain of limitation and declare that nothing will hinder the opportunities God has prepared for me. I decree that promotions, connections, and divine alignments are being released over my life right now, and every demonic barrier is removed in the name of Jesus.

Father, let favor go before me in every place I step. My workplace, my business, my relationships, and my future. Cause my name to be remembered for good. Let unexpected blessings, supernatural breakthroughs, and new opportunities be established in my life. From this day forward, I walk in favor, I step into open doors, and I move in the overflow of Your blessings.

~ In Jesus' name, Amen.

Prayer to Break Financial Curses & Prosper Financially

Heavenly Father,

I come before You in the mighty name of Jesus Christ, the God of abundance and provision. Thank You that every good thing comes from Your hand and that You supply all my needs according to Your riches in glory. Today I take authority over every financial curse, every spirit of lack, every cycle of poverty, and every stronghold that has hindered my prosperity. I decree that I will not live in scarcity, but I will walk in supernatural provision and increase.

By the authority of Jesus Christ, I break every generational curse of poverty and sever every financial bondage from my life. I rebuke every spirit of debt, delay, and financial stagnation. I cancel every demonic assignment sent to devour my harvest and block my opportunities. I command every hand holding my wealth, my promotions, and my resources to release them now. I declare that my finances are loosed from the grip of the enemy and restored into my hands in full measure.

Father, let wealth and riches be established in my house and let my life overflow with opportunities, increase, and abundance. Surround me with favor in my work, my business, and my endeavors. From this moment forward, I walk in financial freedom, stability, and divine provision. No more struggle, no more lack, and no more missed opportunities. I step into a season of overflow, prosperity, and supernatural breakthrough.

~ In Jesus' name, Amen.

Chapter 9:

Victory & Breakthrough

"For the Lord your God is the one who goes with you to fight for
you against your enemies to give you victory."

(Deuteronomy 20:4 NIV)

Prayer for Victory Over
Delays & Stagnation

Heavenly Father,

I come before You in the mighty name of Jesus Christ, my Deliverer and Way Maker. Thank You that You order my steps and accelerate my destiny. Today I take authority over every spirit of delay, stagnation, limitation, and setback that has been working against my progress. I declare that my season of waiting without results is over. Every cycle of delay in my life is broken in the name of Jesus.

By the authority of Jesus Christ, I rebuke and destroy every invisible barrier, demonic roadblock, and spiritual chain that has been holding me back. I reject every form of stagnation and refuse to remain stuck in one place. I command every force delaying my blessings, finances, career, marriage, and opportunities to be shattered by the fire of God. I declare that every closed door must open now and every hindrance must be removed. My time of acceleration has come.

Father, release Your favor and let breakthroughs manifest swiftly. I decree that from this day forward, I will move forward, recover lost time, and step fully into my destiny. No more setbacks, no more stagnation, and no more missed opportunities. I step into a new season of rapid progress, divine acceleration, and unstoppable advancement, for my life is aligned with Your will.

~ In Jesus' name, Amen.

Prayer to Recover Stolen Blessings & Destiny

Heavenly Father,

I come before You in the mighty name of Jesus Christ, the Restorer of all things. Thank You that nothing the enemy has stolen can remain in his hands. Today I rise in my spiritual authority and declare that every blessing, opportunity, and breakthrough that has been delayed, diverted, or stolen from me must be returned. I pursue what belongs to me and I reclaim my destiny in the name of Jesus.

By the authority of Christ, I break every chain that has held back my progress. I rebuke every demonic power that has blocked my finances, delayed my opportunities, or hindered my answered prayers. I command every altar, curse, and decree raised against my destiny to be destroyed by fire. I call forth restoration now—every door that was shut will be opened, every connection that was broken will be restored, and every blessing that was stolen will return multiplied.

Father, let Your angels of restoration gather my blessings from the north, south, east, and west. Everything with my name on it, every opportunity marked for my future, and every assignment connected to my destiny is released back into my hands. From this moment forward, I walk in supernatural favor, divine acceleration, and unstoppable breakthrough. I declare that my blessings will not be stolen, my destiny will not be delayed, and my life will overflow with restoration and victory.

~ In Jesus' name, Amen.

Prayer for Supernatural Breakthroughs & Divine Acceleration

Heavenly Father,

I come before You in the mighty name of Jesus Christ, the God of sudden miracles and breakthrough. Thank You that nothing is impossible with You and that every delay has an expiration date under Your power. Today I declare that my season of acceleration has begun. Every chain of stagnation, limitation, and hindrance working against my destiny is broken in the name of Jesus. I decree that I will move forward swiftly, for You are the God who makes a way where there is no way.

By the authority of Jesus Christ, I command every spirit of delay, setback, and spiritual embargo placed on my progress to be destroyed now. I cancel every demonic assignment designed to slow me down and every obstacle blocking my next level. No power of darkness will hold me back any longer, for my breakthrough has been released.

Father, I decree that I will not be delayed, I will not be hindered, and I will not be denied. I step into divine speed, supernatural favor, and unstoppable advancement. From this moment forward, I walk in sudden breakthroughs, rapid progress, and victory. Thank You, Lord, that Your mighty hand is upon me, causing me to overtake, recover, and accomplish everything You have destined for my life. I step boldly into my breakthrough season with confidence, knowing that nothing shall hinder me again.

~ In Jesus' name, Amen.

Prayer for Open Doors
& Supernatural Favor

Heavenly Father,

I come before You in the mighty name of Jesus Christ, my Way Maker and Provider. Thank You that You open doors no man can shut and surround Your children with favor. Today I take authority over every closed door, every hindrance, and every limitation standing in the way of my destiny. I decree that no good thing will be withheld from me, and every blessing, opportunity, and breakthrough assigned to my life is being released now in the name of Jesus.

By the authority of Jesus Christ, I command every locked door to open and every barrier to be removed. I cancel and reject every spirit of delay, stagnation, and rejection working against my progress. I decree that I will walk into divine connections, supernatural promotions, and favor beyond my imagination. Everywhere I go, doors will swing open, opportunities will pursue me, and blessings will overtake me. Let every work of my hands prosper and let Your favor rest upon me like a shield.

Father, I declare that this is my season of access and advancement. Doors of financial increase, business success, divine partnerships, spiritual growth, and breakthrough are open now. From this day forward, I walk in divine favor, supernatural access, and unstoppable blessings. No door assigned to my destiny will remain shut, for I am covered by the blood of Jesus and empowered by Your Word.

~ In Jesus' name, Amen.

Prayer for the Full Armor of God & Divine Covering

Heavenly Father,

I come before You in the mighty name of Jesus Christ, my Shield and Protector. Thank You that You clothe me with power and surround me with Your unfailing protection. Today, I put on the full armor of God and declare that I am completely covered, fully equipped, and ready for every spiritual battle. No weapon formed against me shall prosper, no scheme of the enemy shall prevail, and no attack will penetrate my life, for I am hidden under the shadow of the Almighty.

By the authority of Jesus Christ, I put on the Helmet of Salvation to guard my mind, the Breastplate of Righteousness to protect my heart, and the Belt of Truth to stand firm against every lie of the enemy. I put on the Shoes of the Gospel of Peace, declaring that nothing shall hinder my steps. I lift up the Shield of Faith to extinguish every fiery dart of the enemy, and I wield the Sword of the Spirit, the living Word of God, to cut down every demonic force and destroy every stronghold. I declare that I am covered, equipped, and victorious in Christ.

Father, I decree that I am strong in the Lord and in the power of His might. From this day forward, I walk fully armored and divinely protected. Every battle I face is already won, every attack of the enemy is already defeated, and every scheme of darkness is already destroyed by Your power. I stand fearless, unshakable, and immovable, knowing that I am covered by Your divine hedge of protection.

~ In Jesus' name, Amen.

Chapter 10:

Protection & Authority

"The Lord will keep you from all harm—he will watch over your life; the Lord will watch over your coming and going both now and forevermore."

(Psalm 121:7–8 NIV)

Prayer for Protection Over Your Children & Family

Heavenly Father,

I come before You in the mighty name of Jesus Christ, my Protector and Fortress. Thank You that You are faithful to guard and keep all that is entrusted to You. Today, I lift up my children and my entire household under Your covering. I declare divine protection, angelic guard, and supernatural safety over their lives. No harm, no danger, and no evil shall come near them, for they are hidden under the shadow of the Almighty.

By the authority of Jesus Christ, I rebuke every plan of the enemy against my family. I cancel every attack of sickness, premature death, tragedy, or destruction that has been spoken or planned against us. I break every word curse, every generational assignment, and every spirit of fear that seeks to harm my loved ones. I cover my household in the blood of Jesus and declare that no weapon formed against us shall prosper. Let Your angels encamp around my home, my children, and everything that concerns me.

Father, I decree that my children will grow in wisdom, favor, and strength, protected in every way. No enemy will snatch them from Your hands, and no plague or disaster will overtake us. From this moment forward, I declare that my family is covered, my children are safe, and my household walks in divine security, supernatural peace, and heavenly protection every day.

~ In Jesus' name, Amen.

Prayer for Protection While I Sleep

Heavenly Father,

Thank You that even while I sleep, You never slumber. You are the Watcher of my soul, the Keeper of my heart, and the Defender who guards me through the night. When the world grows quiet and I lay my head down, I rest in the truth that I am not alone, Your presence surrounds me.

Lord, I renounce every fear, nightmare, or dark presence that tries to disturb my rest. In the name of Jesus, I declare that no weapon formed against me shall prosper. I reject anxiety, torment, and unrest, and I welcome Your peace to cover me like a shield. Let every scheme of the enemy be broken, and let Your angels stand guard around me.

Father, calm my racing thoughts and silence the lies that creep in at night. Fill my heart with Your Spirit, and let Your Word be the song that carries me into peaceful rest. Wrap me in Your protection and remind me that I dwell safely under the shadow of Your wings.

I declare that tonight, I will not fear the darkness, for the Lord is my light and my salvation. I will lie down and sleep in peace, for You alone make me dwell in safety.

~ In Jesus' name, Amen.

Prayer for Protection
on the Road & in Travel

Heavenly Father,

Thank You for being the One who goes before me and the One who watches over me wherever I go. You are my Keeper, my Shield, and the steady hand that guides my steps. As I set out on this journey, I place my trust in You, knowing You are faithful to guard me in all my ways.

Lord, I renounce fear, accident, and harm in the name of Jesus. I declare that no danger shall overtake me, no scheme of the enemy shall succeed, and no weapon formed against me will prosper. Surround me with Your angels to protect me on every side, whether by road, by air, or by sea. Let Your presence go before me, behind me, and beside me.

Father, grant me peace on the road and safety in every mile. Steady my mind, sharpen my focus, and keep me alert. Protect those who travel with me and those I will meet along the way. Let every moment of this journey be covered by Your grace, and bring me back home in safety.

I declare that wherever I go, I am not alone. The Lord is my refuge and my fortress, my guide and my guard. In every step, in every mile, I travel under the covering of His hand.

~ In Jesus' name, Amen.

Prayer to Release Angelic Assistance & Divine Intervention

Heavenly Father,

I come before You in the mighty name of Jesus Christ, the Lord of Hosts and Commander of Heaven's Armies. Thank You that You surround me with Your angels and fight on my behalf. Today I call forth angelic reinforcements, divine intervention, and heavenly breakthroughs in every area of my life. I decree that Your angels are guarding me, protecting me, and clearing the path before me so that no scheme of the enemy shall prevail.

By the authority of Jesus Christ, I release warring angels to dismantle every demonic attack, scatter every enemy, and destroy every stronghold blocking my destiny. I command every obstacle standing in my way to be removed and every evil force to be silenced. Let ministering angels bring provision, divine connections, and favor into my life. I declare that the hosts of Heaven are surrounding me now, fighting for me, and enforcing every word You have spoken concerning my life.

Father, I decree that no battle shall be lost, no plan of the enemy shall stand, and no demonic force shall overthrow what You have established for me. From this moment forward, I walk under angelic protection, divine reinforcement, and heavenly assistance. I declare that doors will open, blessings will manifest, and breakthroughs will locate me quickly, for the armies of Heaven are fighting on my side.

~ In Jesus' name, Amen.

Prayer to Strengthen Spiritual Authority & Boldness

Heavenly Father,

I come before You in the mighty name of Jesus Christ, my Rock and my Strength. Thank You that through Christ I have been given power, dominion, and authority over all the works of the enemy. Today I stand firm in that authority and declare that I will not walk in fear or hesitation but in boldness, confidence, and unshakable faith. No enemy, no weapon, and no voice of doubt will prevail against me, for I am backed by the power of the living God.

By the authority of Jesus Christ, I rebuke every spirit of fear, intimidation, and timidity. I cancel every lie of the enemy that says I am not strong enough, qualified enough, or capable enough. I declare that I will not shrink back, I will not be silenced, and I will not run from any battle. I decree that I will move forward in courage, pray with boldness, and act in authority, knowing that the Lord is my light and my salvation. With God on my side, I cannot be defeated.

Father, I decree that I will walk in the fullness of the Holy Spirit with fearless confidence in every assignment and every place You send me. From this moment forward, I declare that I am bold, I am strong, and I am immovable. I walk in unstoppable faith, divine courage, and spiritual authority. No spirit of intimidation, no opposition, and no power of darkness will ever make me turn back again. I am victorious, for the Lord is with me always.

~ In Jesus' name, Amen.

Chapter 11:

Darkness & Deliverance

"The Lord will keep you from all harm—he will watch over your life; the Lord will watch over your coming and going both now and forevermore."

(Psalm 121:7–8 NIV)

Prayer for Deliverance
from Fear of Death

Heavenly Father,

Thank You that in Christ, death has been defeated and the grave has lost its sting. You are the God of eternal life, the One who promises that nothing, not even death itself, can separate me from Your love. I rest in the assurance that my times are in Your hands and my future is secure in You.

Lord, I renounce the fear of death and every lie of the enemy that tries to keep me bound in terror. I declare in the name of Jesus that death holds no power over me, for I have been redeemed by His blood and raised to new life in Him. Fear will not control my heart, and anxiety about tomorrow will not rule my mind.

Father, fill me with courage to face each day in the light of eternity. Replace dread with peace, and despair with unshakable hope. Let the truth of Your Word anchor me, that to live is Christ, and to die is gain, because I belong fully to You.

I declare that I will not live in the shadow of fear, but in the freedom of faith. The Lord is my salvation and my life; I will trust Him with every breath until the day I see Him face to face.

~ In Jesus' name, Amen.

Prayer to Cancel Premature Death & Claim Long Life

Heavenly Father,

I come before You in the mighty name of Jesus Christ, the Giver of Life and the One who holds my days in His hands. Thank You that my life is secure in You and that no power of darkness can cut short the destiny You have appointed for me. Today I take authority over every spirit of premature death, sudden tragedy, and destruction assigned against me or my family. I decree that I will live a long, full, and prosperous life, and every demonic agenda to take me out before my time is canceled in the name of Jesus.

By the authority of Jesus Christ, I rebuke and destroy every hidden trap, accident, sickness, or attack sent to shorten my life. I break every curse of premature death, every demonic decree over my health, and every negative prophecy spoken against my future. I cover myself and my family under the blood of Jesus, declaring that no weapon, no sickness, and no assignment of the enemy will prevail against us. No shadow of death shall overtake me, and no force of darkness will remove me before my appointed time.

Father, I declare that I will fulfill my God-given destiny and walk in divine health, strength, and protection all the days of my life. From this moment forward, I will not die before my time but live to declare the goodness of the Lord in the land of the living. I am covered, I am protected, and I am secured under the wings of the Almighty.

~ In Jesus' name, Amen.

Prayer Against Nightmares
& Demonic Torment in Dreams

Heavenly Father,

I come before You in the mighty name of Jesus Christ, my Protector and Deliverer. Thank You that You give Your children rest and peace in the night. Today, I take authority over every nightmare, every spirit of fear, every demonic intrusion, and every satanic attack that has tried to disturb my sleep. I decree that from this night forward, my sleep will be peaceful, restful, and filled with the presence of the Holy Spirit.

By the authority of Jesus Christ, I rebuke and cancel every demonic assignment sent to infiltrate my dreams. I break every stronghold of torment, fear, and confusion that has been released against me in the night. I bind and cast out every monitoring spirit, astral projection, or demonic visitation that has sought to attack me while I sleep. I declare that every doorway of darkness is sealed shut by the blood of Jesus, and every plan to steal my peace or plant destruction is rendered powerless.

Father, I cover my dream life under the blood of Jesus. I decree that no spirit of torment will touch me, no demonic vision will come near me, and no spirit of darkness will invade my rest. From this moment forward, I will only receive dreams that come from You. Dreams of revelation, direction, and prophetic insight. I declare that my nights are covered, my dreams are protected, and my spirit is at peace. I will sleep soundly, wake up refreshed, and be filled with the presence of the Holy Spirit.

~ In Jesus' name, Amen.

Chapter 12:

Becoming
Whole & Free

"Therefore, if anyone is in Christ, the new creation has come: The old has gone, the new is here!"

(2 Corinthians 5:17 NIV)

Learning to Receive God's Love

Heavenly Father,

Thank You for rescuing me and setting me free. You've carried me through storms I thought I couldn't survive, broken chains I never believed would fall, and filled my heart with a peace that only You can give. Your faithfulness, power, and love are far greater than I could ever deserve, and I praise You for who You are.

Thank You for loving me before I ever knew how to love You. You saw the weight I couldn't explain, the ache I couldn't hide, and You lifted it with gentle hands.

Lord, Help me to live each day with a heart full of gratitude. Remind me of all the ways You have worked in my life, seen and unseen. Let thankfulness shape my thoughts, words, and actions, filling my spirit with joy and becoming a light to those around me.

Help me remember that this freedom is a gift to be lived, not just received. Let my gratitude deepen, not just for what You've done, but for who You are.

You are my strength and my steady light. And I will praise You, not just in victory, but in every quiet step toward healing and wholeness.

~ In Jesus' name, Amen.

Renewal Through the Holy Spirit

Holy Spirit,

Breathe upon me with the breath of heaven. Let Your presence move through the dry places of my soul like a gentle wind after drought. Where heaviness has lingered, lift it. Where light has faded, rekindle it with the fire of Your love.

Take these worn and weary places in me. These aching corners I've tried to mend alone, and renew them with Your touch. Teach me again to let go of what I cannot change, and rest in the wisdom of Your timing. Fill me with quiet strength, the kind that trusts even in the silence.

Flow through my heart like living water, washing away the residue of fear, failure, and shame. Let Your joy rise again in me. Not loud, but steady. Let Your peace take root and grow deep, stronger than the storms that come.

Thank You for Your mercy that finds me, for grace that stays, and for the power to begin again. Let the change You work in me speak of who You are. Let my life become a quiet testimony of a soul made whole by You.

~ In Jesus' name, Amen.

Becoming a Warrior for Others

Heavenly Father,

You have called me not only to stand firm in my own battles, but to rise in prayer and love for those around me. Make me strong not for my own sake, but for the sake of others. For the ones too weary to lift their heads, for the hearts too broken to cry out.

Lord, let me fight for others the way You fought for me, without fear, without end.

Teach me to stand in the gap with quiet courage, to fight not with anger, but with mercy; not with fear, but with faith. When darkness presses in, let me carry light.

Use my life, God, as a shield of love. Let my strength come from Your Spirit alone, and let my victory always point back to Your grace. May those around me find comfort, peace, and healing not because of me, but because I stood in Your name.

Thank You for being my strength, my shield, and my guide. As I fight for others, remind me that I am never alone. Let Your Spirit go before me and Your love surround me, now and always.

~ In Jesus' name, Amen.

Chapter 13:

Restoring My Heart Through Reflection

Restoring My Heart Through Reflection

Life often leaves deep imprints—heartaches, fractured connections, and silent battles that quietly burden our souls. These hidden weights can prevent us from embracing the peace and freedom God intends for us.

Composing a heartfelt letter in prayer is a meaningful way to lay these burdens before God, letting go of what's been holding you back and welcoming His restorative presence.

By engaging in this process, you begin the journey toward healing, placing your trust in God's hands and believing in His power to restore and renew.

Creating Your Letter of Healing Prayer

Start with Prayer
Begin by inviting God into this sacred space. Ask Him to uncover any lingering wounds or relationships in need of restoration. Pray for the courage to be truthful, for the presence of the Holy Spirit, and for wisdom as you begin writing.

Example prayer:
"God, I come before You carrying the weight of my pain. Reveal to me where I still need healing and whom I need to release through forgiveness. Let me see these people and moments through Your eyes, and grant me the strength to place this pain in Your hands."

Be Honest in Your Writing
Bring to mind the individual or experience that brought you sorrow. Address them directly in your letter, even if they'll never read it. Speak from the heart—whether you feel grief, anger, sorrow, or confusion. Don't edit yourself; this is a personal offering between you and God.

Example opening line:
"I was deeply hurt when..." or "It caused me pain that..."

This step is about setting down the weight you've been carrying. Let your words reflect the emotional toll the situation has taken on you—emotionally, mentally, and spiritually.

Welcome God into the Healing
After expressing your emotions, shift your letter toward God. Ask Him to help you let go of your pain and extend forgiveness, even if it feels difficult. Hand the entire situation over to Him, confident that He is able to mend what feels broken beyond repair.

Example transition:
"God, I place this hurt into Your hands. I ask You to bring healing into this area of my life and grant me the grace to release the bitterness I've been holding."

End with Trust and Gratitude
Finish by reflecting on God's faithfulness and thanking Him for beginning the healing process. Express your trust in His plan and your appreciation for His unwavering love.

Example closing line:
"Thank You, God, for easing the burden I've been holding. I believe You are working in me, restoring what was lost. I'm grateful for Your constant love and mercy."

What Comes After Writing

Once you've finished your letter, take a few quiet moments to pray over it. Ask God to meet you in that space—with peace, with healing, with reassurance. You may feel led to keep the letter as a marker of your growth and restoration. Or you might choose to tear it up, burn it, or throw it away as a way to symbolically let go of the weight you've carried and place it fully in God's hands.

Remember, this isn't about fixing someone else—it's about tending to your own heart and deepening your relationship with God. Come back to this practice whenever you need to. Healing doesn't happen all at once, but each time you open your heart, you're moving closer to the peace and freedom God longs to give you.

Thank You for Taking the Time to Walk Through This Process

You've taken a brave and meaningful step toward healing. Whether this is the beginning or one part of a longer journey, know that God sees your heart, hears your prayers, and is with you every step of the way.